Chicago
Blackhawks

Erin Butler

AV² provides enriched content that supplements and complements this book. Weigl's AV² books strive to create inspired learning and engage young minds in a total learning experience.

Your AV² Media Enhanced books come alive with...

Audio
Listen to sections of the book read aloud.

Key Words
Study vocabulary, and complete a matching word activity.

Video
Watch informative video clips.

Quizzes
Test your knowledge.

Embedded Weblinks
Gain additional information for research.

Slide Show
View images and captions, and prepare a presentation.

Try This!
Complete activities and hands-on experiments.

... and much, much more!

Go to **www.av2books.com**, and enter this book's unique code.

BOOK CODE

P 9 5 8 7 2 8

AV² by Weigl brings you media enhanced books that support active learning.

Published by AV² by Weigl
350 5ᵗʰ Avenue, 59ᵗʰ Floor
New York, NY 10118
Websites: www.av2books.com   www.weigl.com

Library of Congress Control Number: 2014951941

ISBN 978-1-4896-3125-1 (hardcover)
ISBN 978-1-4896-3126-8 (single-user eBook)
ISBN 978-1-4896-3127-5 (multi-user eBook)

Printed in the United States of America in Brainerd, Minnesota
1 2 3 4 5 6 7 8 9 0 19 18 17 16 15

032015
WEP050315

Senior Editor Heather Kissock
Art Director Terry Paulhus

Photo Credits
Every reasonable effort has been made to trace ownership and to obtain permission to reprint copyright material. The publishers would be pleased to have any errors or omissions brought to their attention so that they may be corrected in subsequent printings.

Weigl acknowledges Getty Images and iStock as its primary image suppliers for this title.

Chicago Blackhawks

CONTENTS

Introduction

The Chicago Blackhawks have seen dramatic ups and downs over the years. Since 1926 when Major Frederic McLaughlin founded the team, fans have come to know the Blackhawks as a tough and passionate club that plays with great heart. The Blackhawks are famed members of the Original Six, the group of National Hockey League (NHL) teams that played before the 1967 **expansion**, and continue to play today.

Jonathan Toews has been the Blackhawks' captain since 2008.

The Hawks have been an offensive powerhouse for much of their history, consistently producing NHL legends all the while. They have had success despite facing obstacles. After their first Stanley Cup win in 1934, star player Charlie Gardiner died suddenly. The Hawks pulled together and became a closer team. Four years later, goaltender Mike Karakas took the ice with a broken toe. With his teammates supporting him, Karakas led the Hawks to their second Stanley Cup title.

Known for a physical style of play that matches their gritty city, the Hawks are a source of pride for Chicago natives.

Chicago
BLACKHAWKS

Arena United Center

Division Central

Head Coach Joel Quenneville

Location Chicago, Illinois

NHL Stanley Cup Titles 1934, 1938, 1961, 2010, 2013 2015

Nicknames Hawks, B-Hawks, Blackbirds

5 Stanley Cup titles

59 Postseason Appearances

8 Art Ross Trophy Winners

10 Vezina Trophy Winners

History

7 jersey numbers have been retired by the Blackhawks.

When the Blackhawks won their first Stanley Cup in 1934, the entire city celebrated, including the Blackhawks players themselves.

When the Blackhawks were founded in 1926, it was widely assumed that Chicago would be a great hockey city. Major Frederic McLaughlin obtained the rights to the **franchise** and quickly bought the Portland Rosebuds of the Western Hockey League (WHL) and moved them to Chicago. He named them the Blackhawks, a tribute to his infantry division in World War I.

The Blackhawks proved to have been named appropriately, playing the game like warriors. Guided by the hands-on style of McLaughlin, they beat the odds and became champions in 1934 and again in 1938. Unfortunately, they hit a dry spell, missing out on the **playoffs** for 14 of the next 22 seasons. However, after ownership changed hands and players such as Bobby Hull, Glenn Hall, and Stan Mikita joined the team, they won another Cup in 1961.

What followed was an even longer championship dry spell. From 1962 until 2010, the Hawks seemed to come up short time and time again. Their talent, and extraordinary discipline under coach Joel Quenneville, helped them finally win their fourth championship in 2010.

Before helmets were mandatory, even players like the great Bobby Hull had to pay extra attention to flying pucks.

The Arena

The United Center can hold nearly 20,000 Blackhawks fans. This is the third-largest seating capacity for an NHL arena.

From 1926 to 1929, the Blackhawks called the Chicago Coliseum home. This temporary home was replaced by a more permanent one when the Hawks moved into Chicago Stadium in the fall of 1929. They would play in Chicago Stadium for the next 65 years. The arena would come to be well-known as one of the loudest and most well-loved arenas in sports. In addition to Hawks games, it hosted other sporting events, concerts, and even political conventions.

In 1994, the Blackhawks moved to the famed United Center, which was the largest indoor arena in the United States when it was built. Also home to the Chicago Bulls basketball team, the facility is considered state-of-the-art in every way.

The United Center is perhaps best known for its statues. The famous statue of Bulls legend Michael Jordan was unveiled in November 1994, and has since become a Chicago landmark. Retired Blackhawks jerseys hang from the rafters, and Bulls and Hawks memorabilia can be seen everywhere. Walking around the arena in between periods can be compared to walking through a Chicago sports museum.

The bronze statue of Blackhawks legend Bobby Hull was unveiled in 2011 at the north entrance to the arena.

Where They Play

British Columbia **7**

Alberta **4**

3

CANADA

Saskatchewan

Manitoba **14**

Ontario

Washington

Montana

North Dakota

Minnesota **11**

Wisconsin

Oregon

Idaho

South Dakota

United Center, Chicago ⭐ **8**

Iowa

Wyoming

UNITED

Nebraska

Illinois

Nevada **6**

Utah

Colorado **9**

STATES

Kansas

Missouri **13**

California **5**

1

Arizona **2**

New Mexico

Oklahoma

Arkansas

Pacific Ocean

MEXICO

Texas **10**

Louisiana

Mississ

Gulf of Mexico

PACIFIC DIVISION

1 Anaheim Ducks
2 Arizona Coyotes
3 Calgary Flames
4 Edmonton Oilers

5 Los Angeles Kings
6 San Jose Sharks
7 Vancouver Canucks

CENTRAL DIVISION

⭐ 8 Chicago Blackhawks
9 Colorado Avalanche
10 Dallas Stars
11 Minnesota Wild

12 Nashville Predators
13 St. Louis Blues
14 Winnipeg Jets

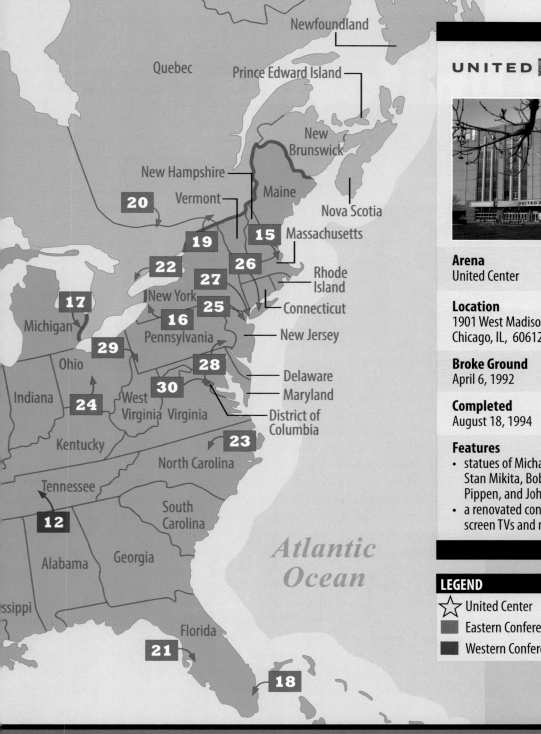

Newfoundland

Quebec

Prince Edward Island

New Brunswick

New Hampshire

Vermont

Maine

20

19

15 Massachusetts

22

26

Rhode Island

27

Connecticut

New York

25

17

16

New Jersey

Michigan

Pennsylvania

29

Ohio

28

Delaware

Indiana

24

30

Maryland

West Virginia

Virginia

District of Columbia

Kentucky

23

North Carolina

Tennessee

South Carolina

12

Alabama

Georgia

Atlantic Ocean

ssippi

Florida

21

18

UNITED CENTER

Arena
United Center

Location
1901 West Madison Street
Chicago, IL, 60612

Broke Ground
April 6, 1992

Completed
August 18, 1994

Features
- statues of Michael Jordan, Stan Mikita, Bobby Hull, Scottie Pippen, and Johnny "Red" Kerr
- a renovated concourse with flat screen TVs and new concessions

LEGEND
☆ United Center
■ Eastern Conference
■ Western Conference

ATLANTIC DIVISION				METROPOLITAN DIVISION			
15	Boston Bruins	19	Montreal Canadiens	23	Carolina Hurricanes	27	New York Rangers
16	Buffalo Sabres	20	Ottawa Senators	24	Columbus Blue Jackets	28	Philadelphia Flyers
17	Detroit Red Wings	21	Tampa Bay Lightning	25	New Jersey Devils	29	Pittsburgh Penguins
18	Florida Panthers	22	Toronto Maple Leafs	26	New York Islanders	30	Washington Capitals

The Uniforms

Players' last names were added to the Blackhawks' jerseys in the **1970s**.

The original Blackhawks American Indian chief design was black and white. In 1935, it became much more colorful.

HOME

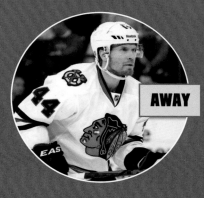

AWAY

The Blackhawks have changed their uniform many times. A key feature of the uniform has always been the **logo**, which is an illustration of an American Indian chief of the Sauk Tribe. The connection goes back to McLaughlin's battalion, which was nicknamed after the chief. McLaughlin's wife, Irene Castle, designed the first logo.

The uniform started out as black and white, incorporating the color red in 1934. Today, the home uniform is red, the away uniform is white, and both uniforms feature stripes with the team colors. Along with the logo, the uniforms also show the letter C crossed with tomahawks, on the shoulders.

Jerseys bearing the names of Blackhawks players Patrick Kane and Jonathan Toews were among the top 10 most purchased NHL jerseys in 2013–2014.

Helmets and Face Masks

Besides wearing a numbered jersey, a Blackhawks player also has his number on the back of his helmet.

In 2014, the Blackhawks added a **"HOCKEY FIGHTS CANCER"** decal to the back of their helmets to support a league-wide effort to raise **CANCER AWARENESS.**

The Blackhawks helmet features a decal of the team's famed logo, which has seen a number of changes over the years. The first design of the logo was a black and white, illustrated portrait of the Sauk Native American chief Black Hawk. Since then, bright colors have been added to the logo and helmet decal, including the iconic multicolored feathers. For home games, the Hawks wear a black helmet, and for away games, a white one.

Blackhawks goaltenders have been very creative with their face masks. One of the most famous masks was worn by Ed Belfour in the 1990s, and it featured the bald eagle as a symbol of leadership and confidence. As a tribute, goaltender Antti Raanta wore a throwback mask similar to Belfour's in 2014.

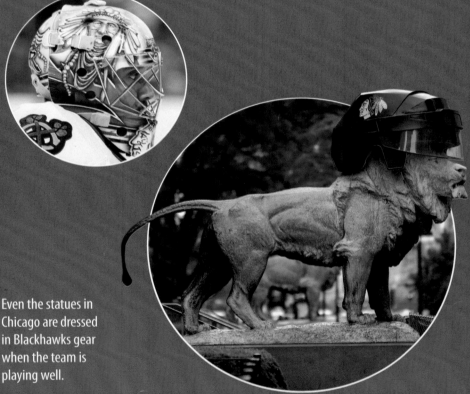

Even the statues in Chicago are dressed in Blackhawks gear when the team is playing well.

The Coaches

29 The Blackhawks have gone through 29 head coaches since their founding.

 Head coach Joel Quenneville is a former defenseman who coaches with the same intensity with which he played.

The Blackhawks have not been the most patient franchise when it comes to coaches. They tend to try out a coach for a short time before replacing him. Though this experimental approach has led to some harsh feelings, it has proven effective in eventually discovering the right person for the job. Hawks coaches who have won have been asked to stick around and truly make their mark.

RUDY PILOUS Rudy Pilous has been involved in the hockey world as both a player and administrator. He had a knack for rallying struggling teams and pushing them beyond expectations. He did this with the Blackhawks as their head coach from 1957 to 1963, leading them to Stanley Cup glory in 1961.

TOMMY GORMAN A lover of all sports, including hockey, Tommy Gorman is known for leading the Blackhawks to their first Stanley Cup title, in 1934. He was also a founding member of the NHL in 1917. He was inducted into the Hockey Hall of Fame in 1963.

JOEL QUENNEVILLE Joel Quenneville has been with the Blackhawks since 2008, and as the current head coach, he has led the team to two Stanley Cup titles. Quenneville has the third-most wins for a head coach in NHL history. Before coming to the Blackhawks, he was a successful coach for the St. Louis Blues and the Colorado Avalanche.

Fans and the Internet

Blackhawks fans show up at the United Center more often than any other NHL fan base does at its own home arena. In fact, in 2013–2014, the Blackhawks led the NHL in average attendance, with 22,623 fans attending nightly.

The Blackhawks fan base has expanded in recent years. During the late 1990s, while owner "Dollar Bill" Wirtz was in control, Hawks home games were not televised. Wirtz felt televising games was unfair to season ticket holders. When Wirtz's son, Rocky, took over in 2007, he decided to televise all games. With this decision, the team's dedication to all of its fans was renewed, not just to those who paid for tickets.

One of the great traditions at the United Center is the sights and sounds of Blackhawks' fans rising, cheering, shouting, and clapping during the national anthem. Together, they create an electric atmosphere and an imposing place for an opposing team to visit. When they are not watching games, fans visit websites such as Second City Hockey, Blackhawk Zone, Blackhawk Up, and the official Blackhawks message board.

Signs
of a fan

#1 In 2010 and 2013, Blackhawks fans showed up in large numbers for the championship parades despite the scorching heat.

#2 Fans love the Blackhawks **mascot**, Tommy Hawk, a large hawk who loves to dance and interact with the crowd during games.

Legends of the Past

Many great players have suited up for the Hawks. A few of them have become icons of the team and the city it represents.

Stan Mikita

A teammate of Bobby Hull, Stan Mikita was another offensive star for the Hawks and led them to their Stanley Cup victory in 1961. Mikita was a brilliant and creative player. He even made alterations to his hockey stick, curving it to improve his shot. Mikita's numerous awards, including the Art Ross Trophy four times and the Hart Memorial Trophy twice, further cemented his legacy. Later in his career, he made a key change to his game by reducing his penalty minutes. His sportsmanship earned him two Lady Byng Memorial Trophies, which is awarded to players who display good conduct. Mikita entered the Hall of Fame in 1983, alongside Hull.

Position: Center
NHL Seasons: 22 (1958–1980)
Born: May 20, 1940, in Sokolce, Slovakia

Bobby Hull

Blackhawks star Bobby Hull, known as The Golden Jet, played for the team from 1957 to 1972 as a part of its "Million Dollar **Line**." Hull was known for his fierce slap shot, which is one reason why he was such a great goal scorer. In 1966, he scored more than 50 goals in a single season, becoming the first NHL player to break the 50-goal barrier. Hull won the Art Ross Trophy for most points in the league three times, and the Hart Memorial Trophy as most valuable player (MVP) twice. He was elected to the Hall of Fame in 1983.

Position: Left Wing
NHL Seasons: 16 (1957–1972, 1979–1980)
Born: January 3, 1939, in Pointe Anne, Ontario, Canada

Glenn Hall

Glenn Hall, known as Mr. Goalie for his outstanding net work, was another Chicago legend from the era of the 1950s and 1960s. He was a unique personality, who was so emotionally into the game that he had a tendency to become sick to his stomach before the first face-off. Hall was a fiercely dedicated goaltender and would go to great lengths to stop the puck. He played 502 straight games in the regular season. Hall won the Vezina Trophy three times for best goaltender, and was inducted into the Hall of Fame in 1975.

Position: Goaltender
NHL Seasons: 18
(1952–1971)
Born: October 3, 1931, in Humboldt, Saskatchewan, Canada

Pierre Pilote

Pierre Pilote rounded out the incredible Blackhawks team of the 1950s and 1960s as a key defenseman. Pilote was tough and showed no mercy on the ice, showcasing his tenacity and defensive skills. After winning the Stanley Cup with the team in 1961, Pilote was named captain. That was a huge honor, considering there were other worthy candidates on the star-studded team. Pilote won the James Norris Memorial Trophy as best defenseman in the NHL three years in a row, from 1963 to 1965. He was inducted into the Hall of Fame in 1975.

Position: Defenseman
NHL Seasons: 14
(1955–1969)
Born: December 11, 1931, in Kenogami, Quebec, Canada

Stars of Today

Today's Blackhawks team is made up of many young, talented players who have proven that they are among the best in the league.

Jonathan Toews

Captain Jonathan Toews is a key playmaker on today's Blackhawks team. He has played with the team since joining the NHL, winning the Stanley Cup with the Hawks in 2010 and again in 2013. Toews is an all-around skilled player with great physical strength, vision, and good skating ability. As captain, he is also a leader. Toews has won the Conn Smythe Trophy as MVP of the playoffs, and the Frank J. Selke Trophy as best defensive forward. On the world stage, he has won two Olympic gold medals with Team Canada.

Position: Center
NHL Seasons: 7 (2007–Present)
Born: April 29, 1988, in Winnipeg, Manitoba, Canada

Duncan Keith

Position: Defenseman
NHL Seasons: 9 (2005–Present)
Born: July 16, 1983, in Winnipeg, Manitoba, Canada

Duncan Keith currently stars for Chicago as an elite defenseman. He has superb skating skills and frustrates his opponents time and time again around the net. In addition, he has great stamina and has repeatedly led the Blackhawks in on-ice minutes per game. Keith has won the James Norris Memorial Trophy as the best defenseman twice, and he made the NHL's first **All-Star** team in 2010 and 2014. He has two Stanley Cup wins as well as two Olympic gold medals with Team Canada.

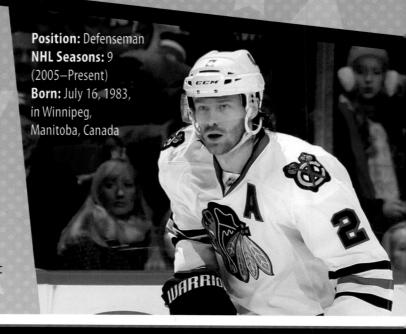

Patrick Kane

Since joining the Blackhawks in 2007, Patrick Kane has consistently posted strong offensive numbers, and his game has grown more complete with each passing season. His skating skills, shooting ability, and playmaking style have been crucial in leading the Hawks back to the top among the league's elite. Kane helped lead Chicago to a Stanley Cup in 2010 and again in 2013. He also played for the United States and won a silver medal in the 2010 Olympics. Kane has won the **Calder Memorial Trophy** and the Conn Smythe Trophy.

Position: Right Wing
NHL Seasons: 7 (2007–Present)
Born: November 19, 1988, in Buffalo, New York, United States

Marian Hossa

Another member of both Stanley Cup–winning teams in 2010 and 2013, Marian Hossa is a strong offensive player who is both quick and difficult to knock off the puck. A seasoned NHL veteran, he has often ranked highly in the league in goals scored. During his career, Hossa has scored close to 500 goals and recorded an impressive five **hat tricks**. The right wing has great puck awareness, and is excellent in all three zones. He is a model of toughness and dependability, characteristics all Blackhawks players are striving for.

Position: Right Wing
NHL Seasons: 17 (1997–Present)
Born: January 12, 1979, in Stará Lubovna, Slovakia

All-Time Records

1,394
Games Played
Stan Mikita set the record for most games played with the Hawks.

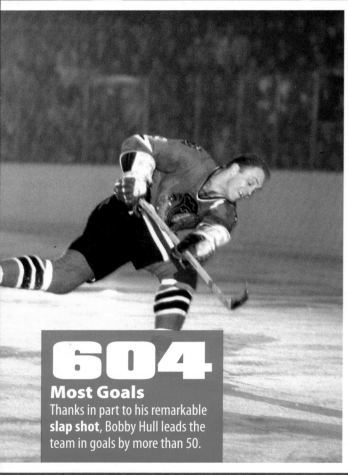

19.4
Shooting Percentage
Darryl Sutter played for the Hawks from 1979 to 1987. During his tenure, he set an impressive record for **shooting percentage**.

604
Most Goals
Thanks in part to his remarkable **slap shot**, Bobby Hull leads the team in goals by more than 50.

418
Wins as Goaltender
Playing for the Blackhawks from 1969 to 1984, star goaltender Tony Esposito shattered the win record.

9,763
Most Saves
Goaltender Ed Belfour recorded an incredible number of saves during his time with the Hawks. He has since been inducted into the Hall of Fame.

Timeline

Throughout the team's history, the Chicago Blackhawks have had many memorable events that have become defining moments for the team and its fans.

1926
Coffee tycoon Major Frederic McLaughlin pays the $12,000 NHL entry fee and creates the Blackhawks.

1926
On November 4, the Blackhawks play their first NHL game. They take on the Toronto St. Patricks at the Chicago Coliseum and leave the ice with a 4-1 victory.

| 1920 | 1925 | 1930 | 1935 | 1940 | 1945 |

On December 15, 1929, the Hawks move to the new Chicago Stadium. Their first game at this location is a 3-1 win over the Pittsburgh Pirates.

1938
Despite having a broken toe, goaltender Mike Karakas leads his team to the Stanley Cup Final and the franchise's second championship title.

1934
Led by goaltender Charlie Gardiner, the Blackhawks sail to their first Stanley Cup win in franchise history, defeating the Detroit Red Wings. Sadly, Gardiner dies two months later.

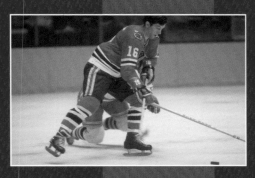

The Future

As the Blackhawks continue to follow a pattern of up and downs, they are currently enjoying an extended upswing. Since breaking their long Stanley Cup dry spell in 2010, they have added another championship title and continue to be a viable postseason threat. Many of the star players from both championships remain on the Hawks' roster, and until they slow down, another championship run is certainly possible.

1961

New ownership in Chicago finally starts to show its stuff as a star-studded team claims its third Stanley Cup title by defeating the Detroit Red Wings.

In 1997, team owner Bill Wirtz dies. The team is taken over by his son, Rocky, and a renewed focus is placed on pleasing the Blackhawks' loyal fan base.

| 1965 | 1975 | 1985 | 1995 | 2005 | 2015 |

2010

The Blackhawks finally snap their 49-year streak without a Stanley Cup title as they defeat the Philadelphia Flyers in the final.

2013

The Blackhawks claim another Stanley Cup title, their second in four years.

Write a Biography

Life Story

A person's life story can be the subject of a book. This kind of book is called a biography. Biographies often describe the lives of people who have achieved great success. These people may be alive today, or they may have lived many years ago. Reading a biography can help you learn more about a great person.

Get the Facts

Use this book, and research in the library and on the internet, to find out more about your favorite Blackhawk. Learn as much about this player as you can. What position does he play? What are his statistics in important categories? Has he set any records? Also, be sure to write down key events in the person's life. What was his childhood like? What has he accomplished off the field? Is there anything else that makes this person special or unusual?

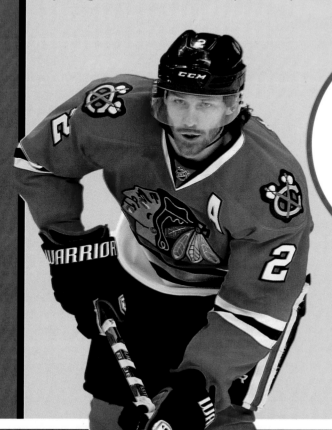

Use the Concept Web

A concept web is a useful research tool. Read the questions in the concept web on the following page. Answer the questions in your notebook. Your answers will help you write a biography.

Concept Web

Adulthood
- Where does this individual currently reside?
- Does he or she have a family?

Your Opinion
- What did you learn from the books you read in your research?
- Would you suggest these books to others?
- Was anything missing from these books?

Childhood
- Where and when was this person born?
- Describe his or her parents, siblings, and friends.
- Did this person grow up in unusual circumstances?

Accomplishments off the Field
- What is this person's life's work?
- Has he or she received awards or recognition for accomplishments?
- How have this person's accomplishments served others?

Write a Biography

Help and Obstacles
- Did this individual have a positive attitude?
- Did he or she receive help from others?
- Did this person have a mentor?
- Did this person face any hardships?
- If so, how were the hardships overcome?

Accomplishments on the Field
- What records does this person hold?
- What key games and plays have defined his career?
- What are his stats in categories important to his position?

Work and Preparation
- What was this person's education?
- What was his or her work experience?
- How does this person work?
- What is the process he or she uses?

Trivia Time

Take this quiz to test your knowledge of the Blackhawks. The answers are printed upside down under each question.

1 What is the name of the arena where the Blackhawks currently play?

A. United Center

2 Who is the current head coach for the Blackhawks?

A. Joel Quenneville

3 How many Stanley Cup titles have the Blackhawks won?

A. Five

4 What is the name of the major who founded the Blackhawks in 1926?

A. Major Frederic McLaughlin

5 When did the Blackhawks win their first Stanley Cup?

A. 1934

6 During what song do Blackhawks fans cheer, shout, and clap loudly?

A. The national anthem

7 What are the Blackhawks' team colors?

A. Red, black, and white

8 Which player was nicknamed The Golden Jet and had a fierce slap shot?

A. Bobby Hull

9 Which player developed a curved hockey stick?

A. Stan Mikita

Key Words

All-Star: a game made for the best-ranked players in the NHL that happens mid-season. A player can be named an All-Star and then be sent to play in this game.

Calder Memorial Trophy: an award given out annually to the hockey player who is considered "the most proficient in his first year of competition" in the NHL

expansion: expansion in the NHL is marked by the addition of a new franchise. The league last expanded in 2000 when the Columbus Blue Jackets and Minnesota Wild joined the NHL.

franchise: a team that is a member of a professional sports league

hat tricks: when a player scores three goals in one game

line: forwards who play in a group, or "shift," during a game

logo: a symbol that stands for a team or organization

mascot: a character, usually an animal, that is chosen to represent a team

playoffs: a series of games that occur after regular season play

shooting percentage: the rate at which a player's shots hitting the net actually go in

slap shot: a hard shot made by raising the stick about waist high before striking the puck with a sharp slapping motion

Index

Log on to www.av2books.com

AV² by Weigl brings you media enhanced books that support active learning. Go to www.av2books.com, and enter the special code found on page 2 of this book. You will gain access to enriched and enhanced content that supplements and complements this book. Content includes video, audio, weblinks, quizzes, a slide show, and activities.

AV² Online Navigation

Book Pages
AV² pages directly correspond to pages in the book.

Audio
Listen to sections of the book read aloud.

Video
Watch informative video clips.

Key Words
Study vocabulary, and complete a matching word activity.

Embedded Weblinks
Gain additional information for research.

Try This!
Complete activities and hands-on experiments.

Quizzes
Test your knowledge.

Slide Show
View images and captions, and prepare a presentation.

AV² was built to bridge the gap between print and digital. We encourage you to tell us what you like and what you want to see in the future.

Sign up to be an AV² Ambassador at www.av2books.com/ambassador.